British Library Cataloguing in Publication Data
Wood, Jakki
In the countryside.
1. Great Britain. Countryside
I. Title   II. Series
941'.009'34

ISBN 0–340–50231–2

Text and illustrations copyright © Jacqueline Wood 1989

First published 1989

Published by Hodder and Stoughton Children's Books,
a division of Hodder and Stoughton Ltd,
Mill Road, Dunton Green, Sevenoaks Kent TN13 2YA

Printed in Belgium by Proost International Book Production

In the Countryside

by Jakki Wood

Mum   Sarah Alex   Peter   Sam   Judy

HODDER AND STOUGHTON
LONDON SYDNEY AUCKLAND TORONTO

One sunny autumn day Mum takes the children into the countryside.

'Follow the green signs,' she says, 'and make sure Judy is on her lead.'

▲ *Winged seeds and leaves of sycamore tree*

The Country Code
1. *Do not start fires.*
2. *Fasten all gates.*
3. *Keep dogs under proper control.*
4. *Keep to paths across farmland.*
5. *Use gates to cross hedges, fences and walls.*
6. *Leave livestock, crops and machinery alone.*
7. *Protect wildlife, plants and trees.*
8. *Take your litter home.*
9. *Help keep water clean.*
10. *Take care on country roads.*

3

Sarah and Alex feel a bit nervous about walking across a field full of cows.

'Keep to the footpath,' Mum tells them. 'The cows are too busy munching grass to bother about you.'

4

Most 'silver top' milk comes from black and white Friesian cows.

Creamier 'gold top' milk comes from beautiful, gold-coloured Jersey cows.

The cows are milked twice a day, once in the early morning and once in the late afternoon.

The next field is full of sheep.
'Oooh, I wish I had a lovely woolly coat to keep me warm,' says Sarah.
'You have,' laughs Mum. 'Your jumper was knitted with sheep's wool.'

6

There are many different breeds of sheep. They are bred for their woolly coats as well as for their meat.

Because they have thick wool coats, sheep stay outdoors all year. Cows are moved into warm cowsheds for the winter.

'Look at all those birds following that tractor,' shouts Peter. 'What are they doing?'

'They're seagulls, eating the worms and insects turned up by the plough,' says Alex.

The farmer prepares the land for winter wheat by ploughing the stubble left from the summer crop into the ground as fertiliser.

These black-headed gulls have lost the dark hood of their summer plumage. All that is left is a black spot behind the eye.

9

'Oh Judy, do stop pulling,' groans Alex.

'She thinks she can smell rabbits,' says Peter.

'Shhh!' whispers Mum. 'She can. Look over there, under that beech tree.'

▲ Beech leaves and nuts

Rabbits live in burrows. They dig the burrows in groups, and each group is called a warren.

Around the entrance to a burrow, the soil is bare, except for nettles or ragwort. Rabbits will not eat these plants.

Trees near the warren may have gnawed bark.

'There are a lot of berries in this hedge,' Sarah says.

'Yes, they're very pretty, but some of them are poisonous,' Mum warns. 'Never touch or eat berries you don't recognise.'

Dogwood berries

Hawthorn berries

White bryony berries

Wild privet berries

These are some of the berries you might find in hedgerows. In winter, berries are an important source of food for birds and small creatures such as mice and bank voles.

'What are those birds doing, Mum?' asks Peter.

'They're feeding on the seeds in those thistle heads.'

'What pretty colours they are,' says Alex.

In the autumn and winter little seed-eating finches have difficulty finding food. So different species flock together to search for seeds.

◀ Goldfinch

◀ Greenfinch

'Birds eat these too,' says Sam.
'So do I!' laughs Peter, filling
his mouth with ripe blackberries.
'Mind the thorns as you pick
them,' warns Mum.

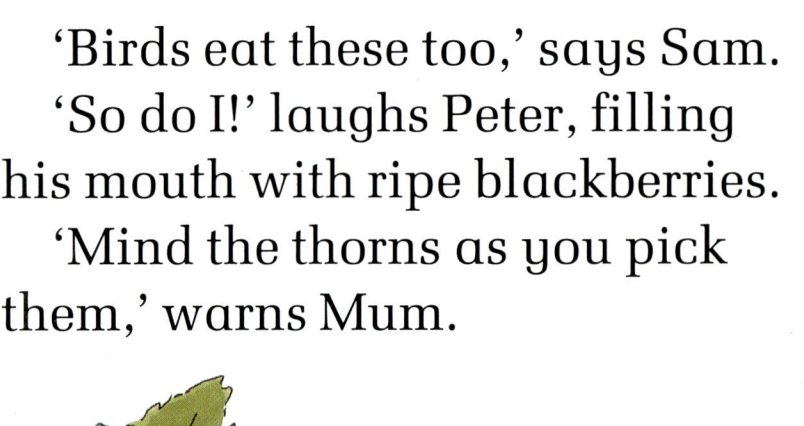

Children and birds are not the only ones who like to eat blackberries. Insects like them, too.

Wasps and flies pierce the skin of the berries to get to the sugary insides. Butterflies may have to wait until the berries are mushy and overripe before they can suck up the sweet juice.

The spider is waiting to trap flies in its web.

Red Admiral butterfly

Comma butterflies

17

'Oh! What's that?' Sarah jumps back as a large screeching bird flies out of the long grass.

'It's a cock pheasant,' Mum says. 'We frightened him.'

Pheasants spend most of the time on the ground searching for grains, leaves and roots in the fields and hedgerows.

They cannot fly for long, but will rise quickly and steeply when in danger. At night they roost in trees where it is warmer and safer.

'Look over here,' calls Mum. She shows the children some tracks left by a badger. Judy sniffs the tracks, then wanders off, still sniffing.

One gap in a hedge or fence may be used by several animals, such as foxes, badgers and rabbits. Look for these clues: fur caught on twigs or barbed wire; paw prints in mud or snow; teeth marks in bark; empty seed or nut shells; animal droppings.

Violet ground beetle

Badger paw prints

Cuckoo pint berries

Hart's-tongue fern

'Judy . . . Judy . . . here girl,' the children call. 'It's getting dark. We're going home.'

But Judy has found a bank vole's grassy nest, under the roots of a hawthorn tree.

Hedges are used to mark the boundaries of fields, to stop cattle straying and to form windbreaks for crop protection.

They also provide homes for many small creatures. These include bank voles, shrews, wood mice, weasels and hedge-hogs, as well as birds, beetles, moths, and hundreds of other insects.

Dog rose hips

Wood woolly foot

Red soldier beetle

Bank vole

'What a noise,' shouts Alex, as a huge flock of rooks flies overhead.

'They're on their way home, too,' says Mum, 'to roost before it gets dark.'

Rooks and jackdaws often come together to form large feeding flocks during colder weather.

Both birds are black, although jackdaws are smaller and have a grey patch at the back of their neck.

Jackdaw

Rook

INDEX